I DREAMED OF FLYING LIKE A BIRD

I DREAMED OF FLYING LIKE A BIRD

MY ADVENTURES PHOTOGRAPHING WILD ANIMALS FROM A HELICOPTER

ROBERT B. HAAS

SCHOLASTIC INC.

New York Toronto London Auckland
Sydney New Delhi Hong Kong

This work is dedicated to dreamers…

To children and adults who chase their dreams in life. When we pursue our dreams, whether to become a schoolteacher or an athlete or an artist, we are living our lives to the fullest. We are setting a lofty goal and pursuing that goal with persistence and strength, knowing that there will be setbacks along the way. The world has been changed the most by dreamers who discovered new lands or created new inventions. Chasing our dreams is the thing that shows we appreciate the privilege of being alive.

And to my family, Candice (my marriage partner for over 40 years) and our three daughters, Samantha, Courtney, and Vanessa, who have all chased their own dreams and helped us to fulfill ours.

And to our magnificent canine clan of six…Oliver, Elmer, Chloe, Henry, Spencer, and Cooper, who only chase squirrels but live a cherished and simple life that we can only dream about.

Contents

THE LANGUAGE OF PHOTOGRAPHY

Very often, we photographers use the language of hunting to describe what we do. "Capturing" or "shooting" means taking a picture. A "shot" means a photo, and a "target" means the animal or other subject we are trying to photograph. But we don't use any type of weapon in our work, and we don't harm the animals in any way. We realize how important it is to leave the wilderness just the way we found it, so the magnificent creatures down below can continue to live their lives undisturbed by our activities.

Introduction

Taking photos from a low-flying aircraft is a thrilling and challenging way to capture unusual images of wildlife and the places where wild animals live. An aerial photographer has all the normal equipment of any other photographer—cameras, lenses, film, memory cards, and other small gadgets. But there is one piece of equipment that is unique—the aircraft. I take my aerial photos from either a helicopter or a very small airplane. Usually, the pilot removes the door next to me so that I can lean out to get the best possible photos. Flying with the door off requires another critical piece of equipment—

a safety harness. I always use two harnesses so if one harness fails, the other one will save my life. Aerial photography is dangerous enough without falling out of the aircraft!

The thrills of aerial photography are many. I am able to fly over deserts, swamps, glaciers, and jungles that few people have ever seen and take pictures that show amazing new ways of looking at the wildlife below and understanding animal behavior.

But the challenges of this type of work are awfully dramatic too! It is extremely cold up there, particularly with the door off. To protect myself, I often wear insulated ski pants, special protective shirts, thick jackets, a face mask, a stocking cap, and two pairs of gloves. But the best way to protect myself is with a great pilot— I depend on my pilot to know the area that I am photographing and to steer the aircraft away from danger. I have faced many dangers in my aerial work, such as being caught in a nasty storm, almost colliding with large birds, and being forced to land in a swamp and in a remote desert. When I am up there shooting away, I know that I have placed my life in the hands of my pilot.

Buffalos and Lions at War

An aerial photographer is rarely able to witness a hunting scene in the wild. The final drama between the animal that is hunting (the predator) and the one being chased (the prey) is usually over in just a few seconds, and often the action is hidden from view by trees or bushes. But one time in Africa, when my pilot and I were flying over the huge Okavango Delta of Botswana, I was able to shoot an incredible hunt.

When my pilot first spotted a large group of African buffalos, the herd was moving slowly through the grass beside a stream. There were no lions in sight at all.

From the air, we were able to see that the herd had a long winding shape and that there were clearly leaders and followers in the group. Soon we noticed a few lions not far from the herd and saw the buffalos react to the threat of the nearby lions by crowding closer together.

Lions and buffalos learn at a very early age to fear and respect each other. Lions will hunt buffalos for the plentiful meat that a buffalo kill provides. But buffalos are not helpless in the face of a lion attack. A buffalo is much larger than a lion and has sharp horns to injure or even kill its enemy.

MORTAL ENEMIES

A fight between a lion and a buffalo is one of the few "fair fights" in the African wilderness. An encounter between them may last for hours before the fighting actually starts. First the lions charge at the herd, then the buffalos charge at the lions. The action goes back and forth. The buffalos on the outside edge of the herd are in the greatest danger of attack since it is too risky for a lion to charge into the middle of the herd, where it would be totally surrounded by its enemies.

We watched the lions and the buffalos charge back and forth at each other for more than an hour, and then we noticed that our helicopter was almost out of fuel. We only had another 15 or 20 minutes left before we would be forced to return to camp. The pilot and I continued to watch the scene down below, but we also kept a nervous eye on the fuel gauge. And then, all of a sudden, the lions made a furious rush at the buffalos, and the herd stampeded away in a cloud of dust.

But one buffalo wasn't fast enough. A lion was able to separate it from the herd and bring it down behind a clump of trees with the help of the other lions. I knew that this dramatic hunt was an incredibly rare event to witness from the air, and I took pictures as fast as I could to capture the action. It ended up a successful hunt for the lions…and a successful photo shoot, but just in the nick of time!

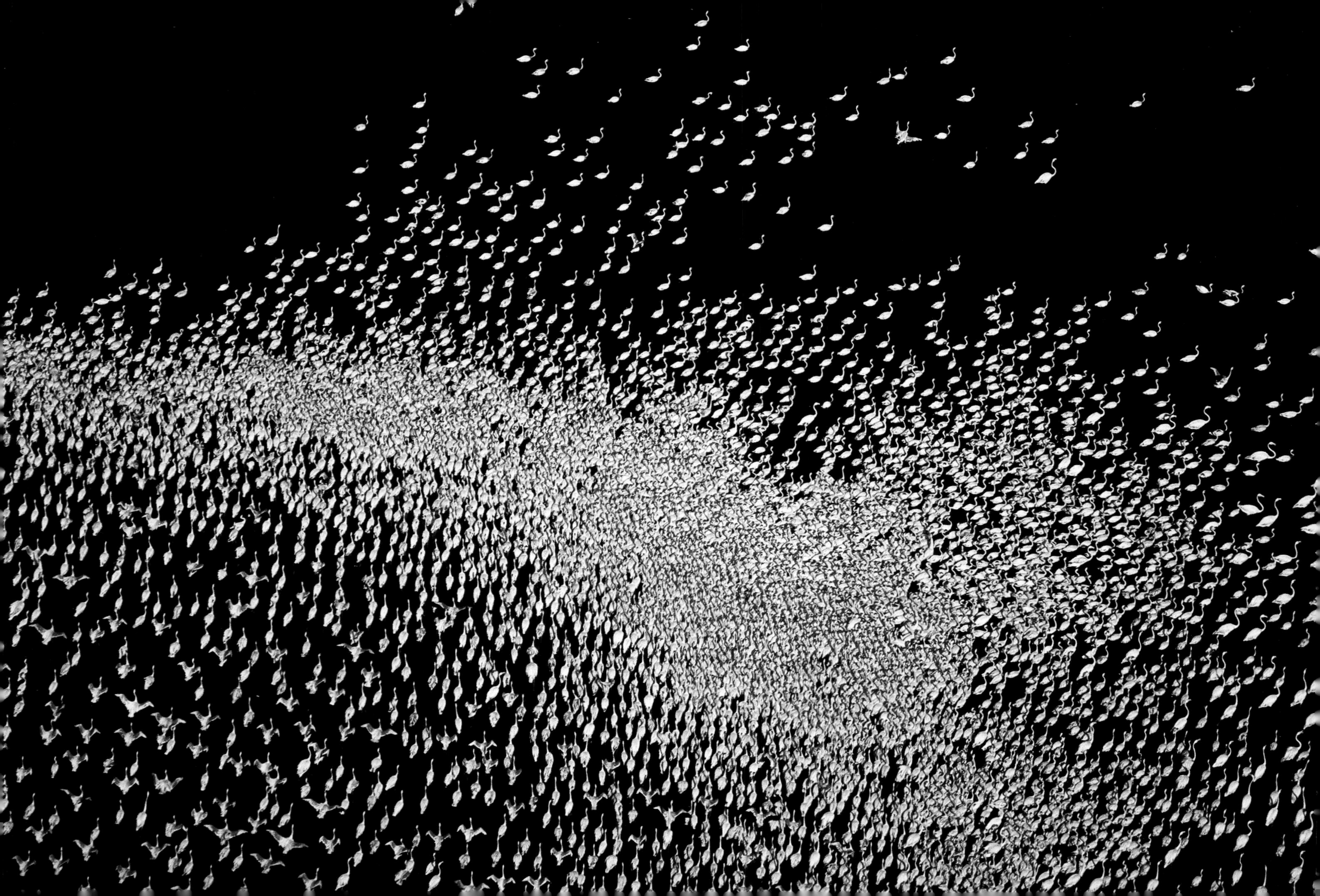

The Miracle of Flamingos

Flying over an area searching for animals, I am always on the lookout for bright colors down below. And there is no sight that is more brilliant in color than the beautiful pink body of a flamingo or, better yet, hundreds of flamingos huddled tightly together in an enormous flock. I have photographed flamingos all over Africa and Latin America, wherever one of their favorite types of food, tiny shrimp, is found in salty ponds and lakes.

Standing far apart from one another, some types of flamingos appear to be more white than pink. But when a huge group masses together, their pink color is much clearer.

WHY ARE FLAMINGOS PINK?

Have you ever heard the expression "you are what you eat"? Well, a flamingo's pink coloring is one way that saying is true. Flamingos are pink because of pink, red, and orange pigments in their food. The pigments that give the flamingo its pink color can be found in two of its favorite foods, algae and small shrimp. The more of these pigments a flamingo eats, the more colorful its feathers will be.

And when a group takes off from the water, you can see the brilliant pink feathers on each bird's wings.

Although their color is what first drew my attention to these spectacular birds, the most amazing thing about flamingos is hard to see without studying aerial photographs. A flamingo's takeoff is just like an airplane's. But while airplanes take off from runways, flamingos perform a natural miracle. They run faster and faster right across the surface of the water before lifting into the sky!

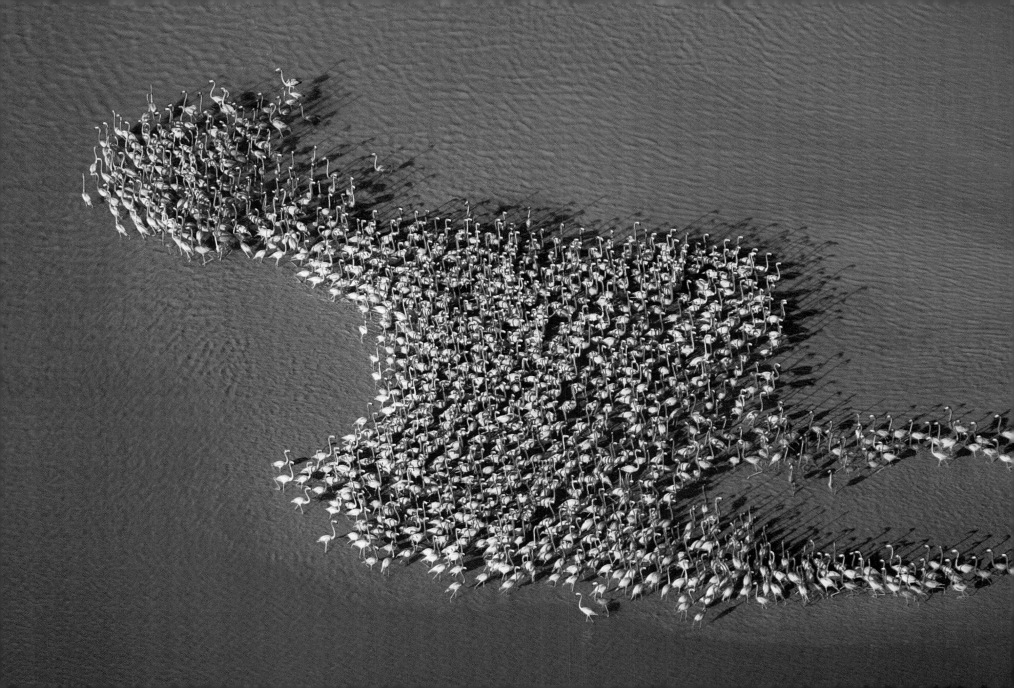

One of the most beautiful sights from the air is a large flock of flamingos moving around in shallow water. The flock forms one shape after another and leaves different patterns as it sweeps across the water. One time off the coast of Mexico, I came across a large flock of flamingos that changed its shape every few seconds, and I kept shooting and shooting for a very long time. And then, when I was just about to leave, I noticed something that was simply unbelievable—the hundreds of flamingos in the flock had actually formed the shape of a flamingo! I was able to capture that shot, and it has become one of my best known photos.

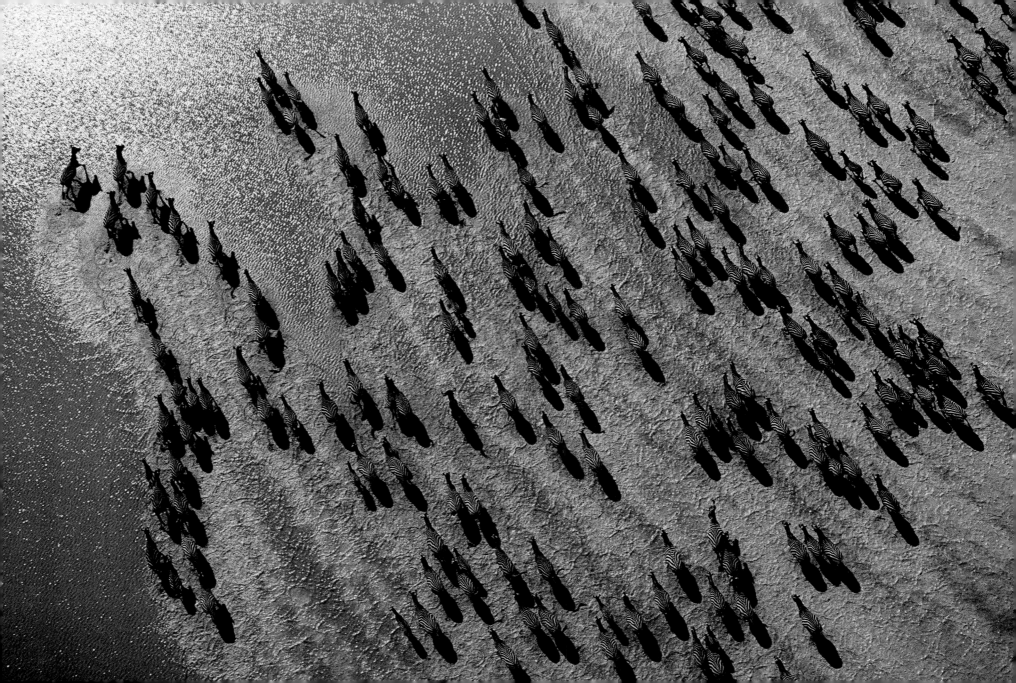

One Wildebeest in a Herd of Zebras

Every morning out in the field, the first thing I do is check the sky to see whether the day will be a good one for photography. High winds and storms are dangerous for flying, and you need sunlight to capture bright colors. On a trip to the salt pans of Botswana, I thought we might never lift off and have a chance to photograph the magnificent creatures that roam this flat ground naturally covered with powdery salt. For the first few days, the pilot and I were drenched with heavy rains that stranded us in our flooded camp. The sound of the rain pounding on our tents was so loud that it was difficult to sleep.

But I knew that the animals were out there splashing through the salt pans in the rain.

At last, our patience was rewarded when we woke up one morning to find that the clouds had vanished and the skies were clear. We dashed out to our helicopter, anxious to find the zebras and ostriches that we suspected were not far away. As soon as the helicopter lifted off, we noticed that the heavy rains had flooded the entire area around our camp and changed the dust of the salt pans into ankle-deep mud.

BANDING TOGETHER

Many animals, from fish to zebras, band together in groups. Sometimes these groups include different animals, such as zebras with gazelles or giraffes with wildebeests. Nobody knows for sure why animals do this, but scientists have many theories. A popular theory is that groups provide protection. With lots of animals on the lookout, large groups can spot predators more easily than a single animal can.

I never would have guessed that the sight of thick mud would make me so happy, but we soon realized that the animals were leaving deep footprints that would allow us to track their movements.

Besides the zebras and the ostriches that we expected to find, we also discovered one wildebeest galloping in the mud. Farther on we found an enormous herd of zebras racing across shallow water. As we looked more closely at the herd, we noticed a very strange sight—right in the middle of the zebras was another wildebeest (just one!) moving along with the herd. We were left to wonder how this one wildebeest had found its way into a large herd of strangers and whether the wildebeest even knew that it was different from the zebras. After all, it grazed on the same food, shared the same enemies, and did not have a mirror to see how different it looked from the striped zebras.

A Close Encounter with Sharks

You might think that a helicopter is a strange place from which to photograph animals that live underwater. Why head straight up when you are trying to take a photo of something that lives straight down? But if you capture a shot of a sea creature at just the right moment, you will have an image that is hard to see from a boat or from the ground. Not only can you photograph hundreds of sea lions crowded around the edge of an island in Alaska, but you can zoom in and even spot their whiskers!

We were once able to

photograph a ray (a large

animal shaped like Batman's

cape) as it glided near the

coast of Mexico. We must

have resembled two birds

in flight—one drifting slowly

underwater and the other

following along just

above the surface.

But photographing sea creatures from the air can be risky. One of our scariest moments came when our helicopter was right over a large group of nurse sharks off the coast of Belize in Central America. The helicopter started to dive much too quickly, and we almost hit the water right on top of the sharks! Fortunately, the pilot was able to gain control, and we escaped unharmed from a close call … with a special image of sharks from above.

TOUGH GUYS

With their big teeth and menacing looks, sharks seem very tough and frightening. Movies often use the fierce appearance of sharks to scare the audience. But in reality, most sharks would never hurt a person. Of the more than 400 types of sharks in the world, only about 24 are dangerous to humans. In fact, we harm sharks much more than they hurt us. Sharks kill only about 10 people each year, but people hunt and kill as many as 100 million sharks. The huge slaughter of sharks every year may even be upsetting the balance of life in our oceans.

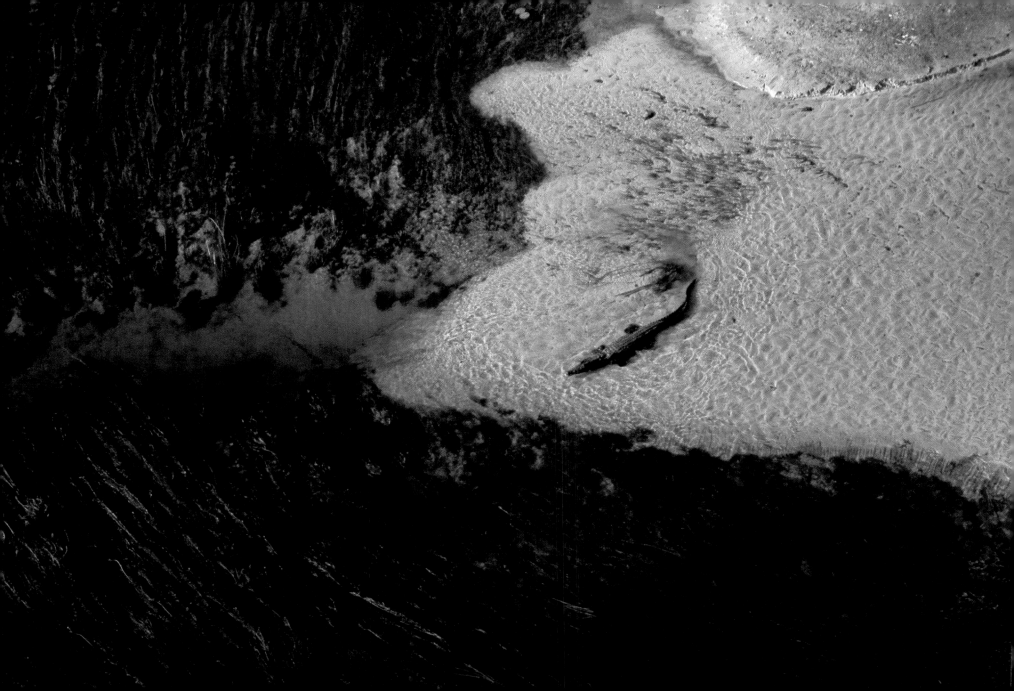

Beware the Crocodile!

No predator is more dangerous than one you cannot see. In the African wilderness, animals risk their lives every day just to get a drink of water. That's because one of their fiercest enemies—the crocodile— lies hidden right below the surface. From the air, the best place to find an African crocodile (or its smaller South American cousin, the caiman) is along the shores of rivers and lakes or on a small island, where the crocodile suns itself and patrols the nearby waters searching for prey.

Even the mighty lions and giant giraffes of Africa are nervous about swimming or leaping across the water—you never know when a crocodile is lurking, waiting to strike. A large stork drinking at the edge of a river in Brazil must be extremely careful when a group of caimans is nearby. Once a crocodile or a caiman spots its prey, it moves silently through the water, grabs its target in powerful jaws, and then tries to drag it underwater and drown it. Once the prey is caught, it hardly ever escapes.

It is very rare to take an aerial photograph of a crocodile after a successful hunt. But once in a while, a croc catches prey that is so large that it takes a long time to eat its entire meal. One day in Botswana, we found a crocodile swimming along the surface with part of a fresh catch still in its jaws. With only a few seconds to spare before the croc dove out of sight, I snapped off a few photos of this very dangerous underwater hunter.

FROM THE AGE OF DINOSAURS

Crocodiles can live as long as 75 years, about the same as a person. But the life span of a crocodile is only a blink of the eye compared to how long crocodiles and their ancestors have survived. The earliest ancestors of crocodiles lived 200 million years ago, at a time when dinosaurs roamed the Earth. The direct ancestors of today's crocodiles evolved about 60 million years ago.

Searching for Giant Whales

I journeyed to the island of Greenland in late summer in search of the great whales that often swim along its coasts. Even as late as August, this enormous icy island in the Arctic is extremely cold. Small icebergs were floating in the chilly seas off the coasts, and the paths that mark where glaciers have traveled were filled with snow and ice.

During the summer this far north, the sun only sets for a few hours each night, so we could fly from five o'clock in the morning until almost nine o'clock at night searching for whales. But photographing whales from the air is a very tricky business—

the sunlight must be very bright to shine through the water, and whales often dive out of sight as soon as they hear the noise of the helicopter.

For the first few days in Greenland, the weather was just so-so. The sunlight was not really bright enough for excellent photos. Even though we worked long hours every day, we were only able to capture a few bits and pieces of the whales—part of one whale's giant head poking through the surface and another one's enormous tail—just above the water.

SPINNING WHALES

Humpback whales, particularly young ones, are curious and playful animals. They frequently raise their flippers and slap the water almost like people do when splashing friends in a pool. They also will roll over, exposing their bellies to the air as if they were spinning. Scientists don't know for sure why whales do these things. The fin slapping might be for communication, and the spinning might be to learn how to control their bodies, but it all might be just for fun.

On our very last day in Greenland, we spotted two large whales swimming close together. As we slowly moved our helicopter into a perfect position over them, one of the whales gave us a chance to capture something I had never photographed before. It spun around upside down and showed us its enormous belly!

Hungry Bears on the Prowl

At the beginning of spring, we headed up to Alaska hoping to spot a few brown bears coming out of their dens at the end of their long winter's nap. During the coldest time of year, when food is scarce, brown bears enter their dens and hibernate all through the winter months, enjoying a long peaceful rest. We knew that if we arrived in Alaska before the bears woke up, there would be none in sight.

But our timing was just right—we immediately spotted a few bears along the snowy sides of the mountains. In fact, we think we were able to photograph one bear on its very first day out of hibernation—there was only one set of footprints that led from the bear's den to where it stood at the edge of a snowy ridge.

A LONG WINTER'S NAP

In the summer when food is plentiful, bears build up their body fat by eating and eating. They can gain as much as 40 pounds in just one week! When winter comes, the bears stop eating and hibernate, using as little energy as possible. In summer, a bear's heart can beat as many as 50 times a minute, but during its winter hibernation it beats as few as eight times a minute. Even though a bear doesn't need much energy when it's hibernating, it does need some, so it uses its fat, which is basically just stored-up food. Mother bears feed cubs born during hibernation with their milk, which is very rich and nutritious, so that the cubs can grow strong enough to survive until the family comes out of hibernation in the spring.

Once the bear is out of its den, it is one hungry beast! It has not eaten all winter long, so it's famished and ready to hunt for food. Although brown bears will eat berries and roots, their favorite feast is the salmon that swim in the rivers and streams in their territory.

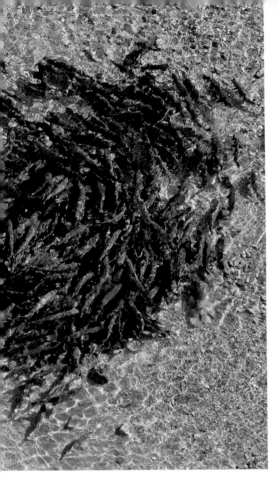

There were hundreds—or even thousands—of fat juicy salmon in each of the streams where the hungry bears were fishing. We noticed that the brown bears were not the only ones who were fishing that day—a man on the banks of the water was poking the shoreline in search of tasty clams buried in the sand.

One bear climbed up on a large rock to get a better view of the salmon down below. Another bear stood in the stream. As one of those big fish swam close, the bear would pounce and try to grab the salmon in its powerful jaws. Sometimes two or even three bears chased the same salmon.

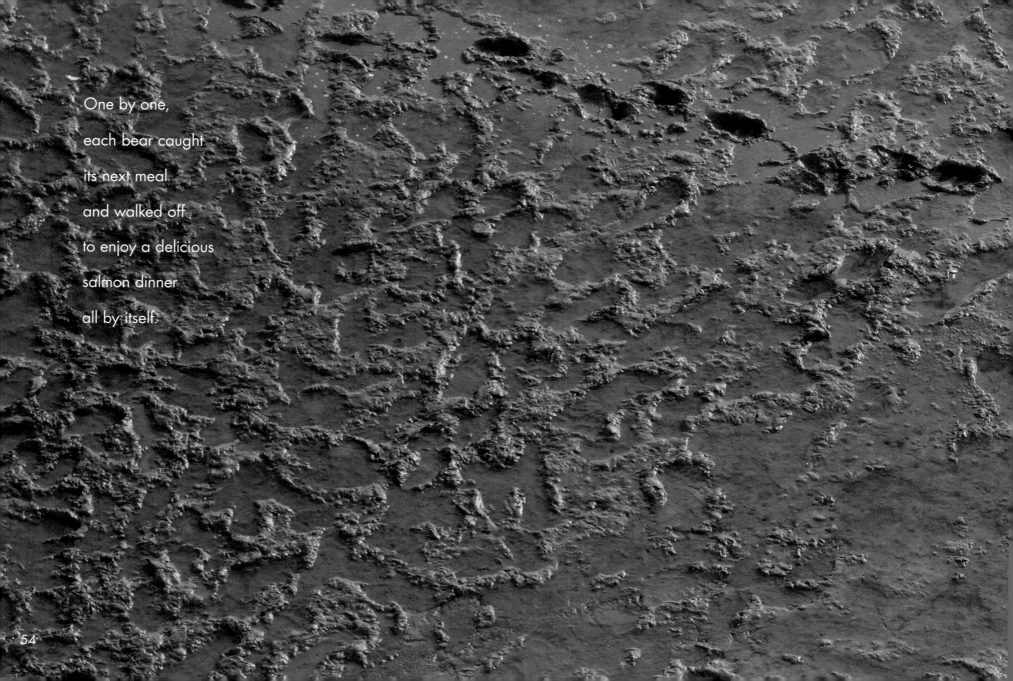

One by one,

each bear caught

its next meal

and walked off

to enjoy a delicious

salmon dinner

all by itself.

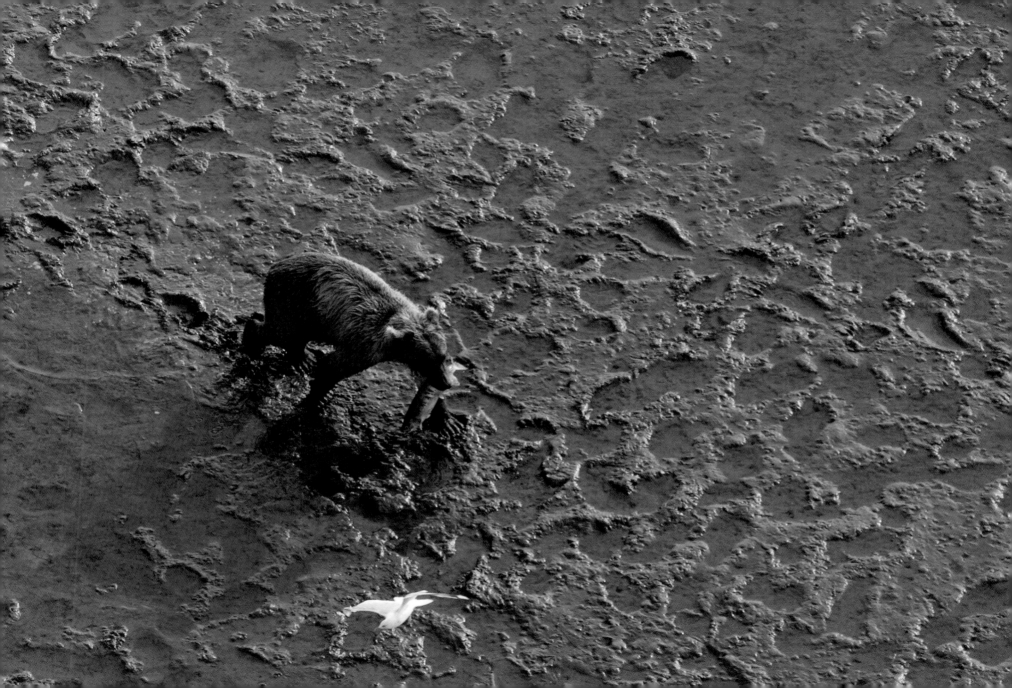

A Dream Come True

Ever since I was a young boy, I have dreamed of flying like a bird. Aerial photography has allowed my dream to come true. With a helicopter, I can join a winged creature or an entire flock in flight and photograph it from above or by its side. When I took a photo of this enormous marabou stork over Ethiopia, it was almost as if I were a stork too, flying right on top of it. And when a large group of flamingos glided past our helicopter, I felt like part of the flock.

In the jungles of Brazil, we cruised beside two beautiful hyacinth macaws. And over the mudflats of Venezuela, a flock of brilliant scarlet ibises passed just beneath our helicopter.

ON THE BRINK

The white-tailed eagle—the fourth largest eagle in the world—is a powerful predator. But that doesn't mean it's safe from humans. Only about 35 years ago, white-tailed eagles were endangered and in need of protection because so many had been poisoned by pollution or shot by farmers who thought the eagles attacked and ate their animals. In 1973, when there were only about 100 pairs of white-tailed eagles left in all of Greenland, the government passed a law protecting them. Because of this law and other conservation efforts to protect it, the white-tailed eagle has made a strong comeback—there are now between 200 and 500 pairs in the skies over Greenland.

Even in the skies, though, there are predators and prey. The white-tailed eagles that patrol the skies in the Arctic are a danger to smaller birds that make a tasty meal.

When I stop to think about it, I realize I am a lot like that white-tailed eagle. We both glide above the Earth searching for something to capture. The eagle hopes to find the prey that allows it to feed itself and perhaps bring back a meal to share with its young. And I hope to capture from the air exactly what I am looking for—a group of special images to bring back and share with my readers.

Glossary

Aerial from or in the air

Algae simple organisms that mainly live in water and use sunlight to produce their food

Conservation efforts to protect something from destruction

Delta the triangle-shaped land at the end of a river

Endangered at risk of being destroyed

Gauge a device that measures how much of something (fuel, water, oil) is in a tank

Harness a piece of safety equipment that holds or fastens a person or object in place to prevent it from falling

Herd a group of similar animals that eat and move around together; usually refers to animals that only eat plants, such as cows

Hibernate to spend a long period of time in conditions where all your bodily functions, such as heart rate and breathing, slow way down, allowing you to conserve energy

Insulated covered with or made from special materials that keep heat from escaping or entering

Mass to gather or come together in a large group

Mortal deadly or dangerous

Pigment a substance that gives things their color

Predator an animal that lives by catching and eating other animals

Prey an animal that serves as food for another animal

Salt Pan flat land covered in salt and other minerals

Theory a scientific explanation supported by facts

Track to follow an animal, sometimes using footprints and other clues the animal left behind

Resources

FROM THE AUTHOR:

African Critters
In his first book for children, author Robert Haas takes his readers on safari in Africa to photograph lions, rhinos, hyenas, and other savanna animals.

FROM THE HUMANE SOCIETY OF THE UNITED STATES:

Kindnews.org
This website is a rich resource if you're interested in how you can help animals around the world.

FROM NATIONAL GEOGRAPHIC:

National Geographic Kids website has cool animal facts, pictures, sounds, and videos. http://kids.nationalgeographic.com/animals

National Geographic Kids Magazine
Featuring tons of animal stories, photos, and weird facts, this magazine is perfect for animal lovers.

National Geographic Encyclopedia of Animals
This 256-page reference book with over 1,000 illustrations and photographs introduces kids to the rich variety of the animal world.

Face to Face with Animals
In this series, National Geographic photographers give kids an up-close-and-personal introduction to their favorite animals. Included are:

Face to Face with Butterflies by Darlyne Murawski
Face to Face with Caterpillars by Darlyne Murawski
Face to Face with Cheetahs by Chris Johns
Face to Face with Dolphins by Flip and Linda Nicklin
Face to Face with Elephants by Beverly and Dereck Joubert
Face to Face with Frogs by Mark Moffett
Face to Face with Gorillas by Michael "Nick" Nichols
Face to Face with Grizzlies by Joel Sartore
Face to Face with Leopards by Beverly and Dereck Joubert
Face to Face with Lions by Beverly and Dereck Joubert
Face to Face with Manatees by Brian Skerry
Face to Face with Orangutans by Tim Laman and Cheryl Knott
Face to Face with Penguins by Yva Momatiuk and John Eastcott
Face to Face with Polar Bears by Norbert Rosing
Face to Face with Sharks by David Doubilet and Jennifer Hayes
Face to Face with Whales by Flip and Linda Nicklin
Face to Face with Wild Horses by Yva Momatiuk and John Eastcott
Face to Face with Wolves by Jim Brandenburg

GREAT PLACES TO LEARN ABOUT ANIMALS ON THE WEB:

The National Audubon Society
http://www.audubon.org/educate/kids

The San Diego Zoo
http://www.sandiegozoo.org/kids/index.html

Index

Illustrations are indicated by **boldface.**

Cover design by Lisa Lytton.

Text and photographs copyright © 2010 by Robert B. Haas.
Compilation copyright © 2010 by National Geographic Society.
Cover copyright © 2010 by National Geographic Society.
All rights reserved. Published by Scholastic Inc., 557 Broadway, New York, NY 10012, by arrangement with National Geographic Society.
Printed in the U.S.A.

ISBN-13: 978-0-545-57957-5
ISBN-10: 0-545-57957-0

13 14   40   22 21 20